the
CRUCIFIED
LIFE

SEVEN
WORDS
FROM
THE
CROSS

FORGIVENESS | SALVATION | RELATIONSHIP | DISTRESS | ABANDONMENT | REUNION | TRIUMPH

CONTENTS

SESSIONS

APPENDICES

SMALL GROUP LEADERS

ENDORS

Charlie Holt brings us to the foot of the cross and the very heart of the Christian gospel. He invites us to ponder the death of Jesus for us and our own death to self in response to him. Powerful, compelling, transformative; a wonderful study for Lent or any other time.

The Rt. Rev. John W. Howe, Retired Bishop of the Diocese of Central Florida

The Christian Life Trilogy is masterfully written to tie in both an excellent small group curriculum and challenging daily devotion. This curriculum is a must for all churches desiring to have Jesus' life, death, and resurrection impact the way they go about their daily work and life. If you're a church who follows the traditional church calendar…it's a no-brainer to let this excellent curriculum guide you through Lent, Easter, and Pentecost in a way you have never experienced before!

The Rev. Wes Sharp, Discipleship Priest, St. Peter's Episcopal Church, Lake Mary, FL

Many people write on topics of which they have little to no experience. Charlie Holt is different. He writes of evangelism as a result of growing a congregation. What he shares is the real deal!

The Rt. Rev. Jay Lambert, Bishop of the Diocese of Eau Claire

Charlie is a gifted teacher and his passion for the Scripture brings the Word alive for all. His enthusiasm for helping others grow in faith, his compassion for God's people and his deeply rooted relationship with Jesus makes him an ideal person to create and share this transforming work.

The Ven. Kristi Alday, Archdeacon of the Diocese of Central Florida

Father Charlie Holt's series *The Crucified Life* offers all Christians not only a profound study of Scripture, but even more importantly a direct and practical means of applying the eternal truths of Christ's death and Resurrection to meet the challenges and frustrations of daily life.

Roni H.

In his series, Father Charlie Holt offers believing Christians new reflections on the sublime lessons of Christ's sacrifice for us, while at the same time offering means whereby we as individuals can apply the lessons of Calvary to our own lives. The series is an important opportunity to grow in faith by means of encouragement and meditation, especially as regards the self-examination that all Christians are called upon to do in our walk.

Martha Hoeber

I have attended many of Father Charlie's wonderful classes on the workings and the words of the LORD, and I believe there is no one more qualified nor one more driven through guidance of The Holy Spirit than Charlie Holt. For those of us who love the Bible, his ability to sort out complicated issues into meaningful and straightforward application is unparalleled.

Jim Grisham

I've been taught that a Godly vision is born out of a recognized need in the people of God. Out of his passion for Christ, Charlie Holt has recognized a need in the people of God to grow together in community through a deeper understanding of Christ crucified, resurrected and ascended. The new small group series, *The Christian Life Trilogy* satisfies that need.

The Rev. James Sorvillo, Rector of the Church of the Ascension, Orlando, FL

Crucified Life: Seven Words from the Cross will open your eyes to the significance and implications for your life of each and every word spoken by our Savior in His last moments on earth. What a blessing this study was for me! Taste this Spirit-led food for your Lenten experience.

Elizabeth Barber

Having already experienced *Crucified Life: Seven Words From The Cross*, I can attest to the incredible impact of these messages from Jesus to us, as explored by Rev. Holt. *The Christian Life Trilogy* will reach into virtually every aspect of your life, ensuring that you will deepen your adoration for The Lord who loves you without end.

Laurie Mealor

ACKNOWL

This project is offered to the glory of God for the renewal of the Church; and, with gratitude for the following people and organizations for their support and participation in this project:

Mrs. Brooke Holt
Mr. Matthew Ainsley
The Ven. Kristi Alday
The Rev. Wally Arp
The Rev. Jabriel S. Ballentine
Mr. Josh Bales
Mrs. Elizabeth Barber
Mr. Brian Bolton
Mrs. Nina Bolton
Ms. Helen Bostick
Mr. Robert Boarders
The Rev. Sarah Bronos
Mr. F. Scott Brown
Mrs. Candy Brown
Miss Lizzy Sult Case
The Rev. Sonia Sullivan Clifton

Mr. Dalas Davis
Mr. Samuel Dunaway
Mrs. Jenna Dunaway
Mr. John Gullett
Mrs. Martha Hoeber
The Rev. Canon Justin Holcomb
Mrs. Colette Ivanov
Ms. Kathy Krasnoff
Mrs. Laurie Mealor
Ms. Virginia Mooney
Mr. James Nedved
The Rev. Canon Tim Nunez
Mrs. Ada O'Neil
The Rev. Andrew Petiprin
Mr. Gordon Sims
The Rev. Jim Sorvillo

OGEMENTS

Mrs. Heather Startup
Mr. Joe Thoma
Mr. Jarda Tusek
Mrs. Sarah Tusek
Mr. David Wellday
Mr. Todd Wilson
Mrs. Sharon Wilson
Mr. Lemar Williams
Mrs. Karen Williams
Mrs. Susie Millonig
The Rev. Dane Wren
The Very Rev. Anthony Clark
St. Peter's Episcopal Church in Lake Mary, FL
The Cathedral Church of St. Luke, Orlando, FL
Allen White & Lifetogether Ministries, Inc.

FOREWORD

The Reverend Charlie Holt has greatly expanded the traditional "Seven last words from the cross" into an extraordinary and deep Lenten Group Bible Study program. With depth of research and breadth of material, Fr. Holt has compiled a body of work which will be helpful and timely for years to come. Rather than exploring the words from the cross only on Good Friday, the author uses these timeless passages as a framework for all of Lent. Fr. Holt includes supplemental material from hymns, works of art, and other helpful illustrations. All of this is held together with well-thought-out exposition from the author's considerable Biblical knowledge. When Good Friday arrives, the reader is prepared for this most solemn day of the Church Year.

Father Holt's writings display the work of a person of faith who is also a theologian and Biblical scholar. He is a frequent contributor to the ongoing concerns and issues of the current church. His writings are important to the debates about Church and culture. His writing is refreshingly clear and direct. His teaching not only follows the received tradition of the Church but also reflects the Old Testament understanding of prophetic discourse. He calls The Church back to the covenantal roots of the faith, rather than encouraging trendy and innovative theology.

This study, well suited for individual and for small group use is refreshing, solid, enlightening and deeply Christ-centered. One only hopes that there will be future offerings from this gifted priest and author.

+Francis C. Gray
Retired Bishop of Northern Indiana

WEL<

Welcome to *The Crucified Life*. Over the next seven weeks, you will experience the joy of life in community as you come together to listen, discuss, reflect and grow together in your lives of faith.

When God created the world, He pronounced His creation "good," with one exception: man's being alone. Being alone was "not good," said God. We as human beings need each other. Jesus called 12 disciples to come alongside Him during His earthly ministry. We are designed for community, to live our lives alongside and in companionship with others. In the context of community, we connect with one another and with God in life-changing ways.

This unique small group curriculum will give you the opportunity to hear in-depth Biblical teaching and then openly discuss that teaching in your group, wrestling together with God's Word and providing mutual support as you allow your life to be transformed by what you discover. The curriculum is designed to connect your weekly small group study with your individual daily times with God, as well as what you hear in church each week.

This Lenten curriculum is centered on a DVD teaching series focused on the Seven Last Words spoken by Christ on the cross. There are seven unique teaching sessions, one for each lesson. In your small group, you will watch the DVD teaching together, then dig deeper through the Scriptures and questions provided. Each week, you will discover how the Scriptures and homilies you experience in church are related to the small group teaching.

At the end of each session in this study guide, you'll be referred to the corresponding Daily Devotions in *The Crucified Life* book for the upcoming week. These Devotions will help you further explore what the

COME

weekly teaching means for your life. There's also a Scripture verse we hope you will commit to memory, as well as a place to record your own personal reflections.

We trust that *The Crucified Life* curriculum will provide a positive introduction to small group community for those who are new, as well as a rich and rewarding experience to those who are veterans of small groups.

In all of this, our prayer is that you would experience God and the truths of the Scriptures in a powerful new way as you take part in this small group study.

INVITATION

The Call to a Holy Lent

DEAR PEOPLE *of* GOD

The first Christians observed with great devotion the days of our Lord's Passion and Resurrection, and it became the custom of the Church to prepare for them by a season of penitence and fasting. This season of Lent provided a time in which converts to the faith were prepared for Holy Baptism.

It was also a time when those who, because of notorious sins, had been separated from the body of the faithful were reconciled by penitence and forgiveness, and restored to the fellowship of the Church. Thereby, the whole congregation was put in mind of the message of pardon and absolution set forth in the Gospel of our Savior, and of the need which all Christians continually have to renew their repentance and faith.

I invite you, therefore, in the name of the Church, to the observance of a holy Lent by self-examination and repentance; by prayer, fasting, and self-denial; and by reading and meditating on God's holy Word. And, to make a right beginning of repentance, and as a mark of our mortal nature, let us now kneel before the Lord, our Maker and Redeemer. --The Book of Common Prayer (BCP), p. 264-65

This Lent, you are invited to take a journey into the heart of the *Crucified Life.* Jesus challenged his disciples more than once to "pick up your cross and follow me."

Jesus said, "If anyone would come after me, he must deny himself and take up his cross daily and follow me." – LUKE 9:23 (ESV)

Notice the word "daily," which is included in the verse from Luke's Gospel. Taking up our cross daily does not mean literally dying every day, of course. It is appointed for us to physically die on one appointed day. However, Jesus calls his followers to a daily discipline and focus on self-denial illustrated by the image of "taking up the cross."

The period of Lent is a 40-day journey of self-denial. Through "self-examination and repentance; by prayer, fasting, and self-denial; and by reading and meditating on God's holy Word," (Book of Common Prayer, p. 265) we are invited by the Church and the Lord to individually and corporately prepare ourselves for the annual celebration of the death and resurrection of Jesus during Holy Week and Easter. This is accomplished through a concentrated time period of "taking up our cross."

The 40-day period begins with the service of Ash Wednesday. Here we acknowledge our finite and mortal nature. "Remember that you are dust, and to dust you shall return." As these words are spoken, the ashes are applied to our foreheads in the Sign of the Cross. As disciples, we are marked for crucifixion—taking up our own cross.

The four Gospel witnesses—Matthew, Mark, Luke, and John—testify that Jesus spoke seven distinct times from the cross:

Traditionally, these seven sayings have been associated with seven words: (1) Forgiveness; (2) Salvation; (3) Relationship; (4) Distress; (5), Abandonment; (6) Reunion; and (7) Triumph.

Each week of the Lenten season, we will reflect on one of Jesus' seven last utterances from the cross. The seven last sayings of Jesus are jewels of great value, and worthy of our gaze, deep meditation, and reflection.

My prayer during this Lent is that you and I will walk daily toward the cross with humility and purpose. I look forward to seeing how God will use this offering of ourselves to Him.

I pray that your small group meeting time will be a blessing, leading to personal and corporate growth. Each day I will offer a focused reflection on one aspect of that week's saying in *The Crucified Life* devotional book.

Please let me or any of the other clergy in your life know how we may serve you in this season of your spiritual growth in Christ Jesus our Lord. As I am faithfully yours in Him,

"Father, forgive them, for they know not what they do."
– LUKE 23:34 (ESV)

"Truly I say to you, today you will be with Me in Paradise."
– LUKE 23:43 (ESV)

"Woman, behold your son... Behold your mother."
– JOHN 19:26-27 (ESV)

"I thirst."
– JOHN 19:28 (ESV)

"My God, my God, why have you forsaken me?"
– MATTHEW 27:46

"Father, into your hands I commit my spirit."
– LUKE 23:46

"It is finished."
– JOHN 19:30

Charlie +

Almighty God, whose most dear Son went not up to joy but first he suffered pain, and entered not into glory before he was crucified: Mercifully grant that we, walking in the way of the cross, may find it none other than the way of life and peace; through Jesus Christ our Lord. Amen. (BCP, p. 99.)

USING *this* WORKBOOK

Tools to Help You Have a Great Small Group Experience

1 Notice the Table of Contents is divided into three sections: (1) Sessions; (2) Appendices; and (3) Small Group Leaders. Familiarize yourself with the Appendices. Some of them will be used in the sessions themselves.

2 If you are facilitating/leading or co-leading a small group, the section Small Group Leaders will offer you some hard-learned insights from the experiences of others that will encourage you and help you avoid common obstacles to effective small group leadership.

3 Use this workbook as a guide, not a straitjacket. If the group responds to the lesson in an unexpected but honest way, go with that. If you think of a better question than the next one in the lesson, ask it. Take to heart the insights included in the Frequently Asked Questions pages and the Small Group Leaders section.

4 You may find that you can't get through all the questions in a given lesson in the time you have. Look for the questions marked with an asterisk, and use those first if you're short on time.

5 Enjoy your small group experience.

6 Pray before each session—for your group members, for your time together, for wisdom and insight.

7 Read the Outline for Each Session on the next pages so that you understand how the sessions will flow.

OUTLINE *for* EACH SESSION

A typical group session for The Crucified Life study will include the following sections:

WEEKLY MEMORY VERSES. Each session opens with a Memory Verse that emphasizes an important truth from the session. This is an optional exercise, but we believe that memorizing Scripture can be a vital part of filling our minds with God's truth for our lives. We encourage you to give this important habit a try. The verses for our seven sessions are also listed in the appendix.

SHARE YOUR STORY. The foundation for spiritual growth is an intimate connection with God and His family. You build that connection in part by sharing your story with a few people who really know you and who earn your trust. This section includes some simple questions to get you talking—letting you share as much or as little of your story as you feel comfortable doing. Each session typically offers you two options. You can get to know your whole group by using the icebreaker question(s), or you may also desire to check in with one or two group members, in between weekly sessions, for a deeper connection and encouragement in your spiritual journey.

HEAR GOD'S STORY. In this section, you'll read the Biblical passages and listen to teaching—in order to better understand God's story of creation and redemption and discover how your story connects to the larger story of the Bible. When the study directs you, you'll turn on the DVD and watch a short

teaching segment. You'll then have an opportunity to read a passage of Scripture and discuss both the teaching and the text. You'll be gleaning new insights from God's Word, and then discussing how you should live in light of these truths. We want to help you apply the insights from Scripture practically and creatively, from your heart as well as your head. At the end of the day, allowing the timeless truths from God's Word to transform our lives in Christ should be your greatest aim.

STUDY NOTES. This brief section provides additional commentary, background or insights into the passage you'll study in the *Hear God's Story* section.

CREATE A NEW STORY. God wants you to be a part of His Kingdom—to weave your story into His. That will mean change. It will require you to go His way rather than your own. This won't happen overnight, but it should happen steadily. By making small, simple choices, we can begin to change our direction. This is where the Bible's instruction to be "doers of the Word, not hearers only" (James 1:22, ESV) comes into play. Many people skip over this aspect of the Christian life because it can be frightening, difficult, relationally awkward or simply too much work for our busy schedules. But Jesus wanted all of His disciples to know Him personally, carry out His commands, and help outsiders connect with Him. This doesn't necessarily mean preaching on street corners. It could mean welcoming newcomers, hosting a short-term group in your home, or walking through this study with a friend. In this study, you'll have an opportunity to go beyond Bible study to Biblical living. This section will also have a question or two that will challenge you to live out your faith by serving others, sharing your faith, and worshiping God.

FOR ADDITIONAL STUDY. If you have time and want to dig deeper into more Bible passages about the topic at hand, we've provided additional passages and questions. Your group may choose to read and prepare ahead of each meeting in order to cover more Biblical material. If you prefer not to do study homework, this section will provide you with plenty to discuss within the group. These options allow individuals or the whole group to expand their study while still accommodating those who can't do homework or are new to your group. You can discuss this in your group or just study it on your own, whatever your group prefers.

DAILY DEVOTIONS. Each week under the heading Daily Devotions, we refer you to the Daily Devotions found in *The Crucified Life* companion book. There is much more to learn and consider in the book *The Crucified Life*, material that is not covered in the small group material. We encourage you to set aside a time each day for these devotions. The practice will give you a chance to slow down, delve more deeply into the weekly teaching and pray through it. Use this time to seek God on your own throughout the week. Try not to rush; take the time to truly ponder God's Word and listen for His direction.

FORGIVENESS

Father, forgive them for they know not what they do.

Bear with each other and forgive one another if any of you has a grievance against someone. Forgive as the Lord forgave you.

COLOSSIANS 3:13

This series, *The Crucified Life*, walks us through Christ's last hours on the cross and offers us not only the opportunity for somber contemplation, but also an invitation to deepen our faith as we consider how we can begin to follow Christ more closely every day. Paradoxically, Jesus calls us to follow Him in the way of the cross as the pathway to eternal life.

Often referred to as the "Seven Last Words of Jesus," Christ's final statements, spoken from the cross, provide us with an opportunity for deep reflection as we consider the grace and redemption His suffering and death brought forth. These last "words" are taken from the four Gospels, and they have been used for two thousand years as a worthy meditation on the nature of the Christian's calling to pick up his cross and follow Jesus (Luke 9:23).

In each of the following seven sessions, we will reflect on one of these last sayings.

In our first session, *Forgiveness*, we will consider:

-       Why is forgiveness so difficult?
-       In what ways do passing the peace and praying The Lord's Prayer
        on Sundays teach us about forgiveness?
-       Why is forgiving others such an important part of following Christ?

In this session, we will look at ways we can more closely follow Christ's example by forgiving. And we'll do it the best way possible—together.

SHARE *your* STORY

Each of us has a story. The events of our life—good, bad, wonderful or challenging—have shaped who we are. God knows your story, and He intends to redeem it. He will use every struggle and every joy to ultimately bring you to Himself. When we share our stories with others, we give them the opportunity to see God at work.

When we share our stories, we realize we are not alone; we have common experiences and thoughts. Your story can encourage someone else, and telling it can be a path to freedom for you and for those with whom you share it.

Open your group with prayer. This should be a brief, simple prayer, in which you invite God to be with you as you meet. You can pray for specific requests at the end of the meeting, or stop momentarily to pray if a particular situation comes up during your discussion.

If you prefer, you could use a collect from the Book of Common Prayer to begin your time together, such as:

Almighty God, whose most dear Son went not up to joy but first he suffered pain, and entered not into glory before he was crucified: Mercifully grant that we, walking in the way of the cross, may find it none other than the way of life and peace; through Jesus Christ our Lord. Amen (BCP, p. 99.).

As you begin, pass around a copy of the *Small Group Roster* on page 146. Have everyone introduce themselves, then write down their contact information. Ask someone to make copies or type up a list with everyone's information and email it to the group during the week.

Then, begin your time together by using the following questions and activities to get people talking.

1.   What brought you here? What do you hope to get out of this group?

2.   Why do people find it difficult to forgive someone who wrongs them?

3.   Whether your group is new or ongoing, it's always important to reflect on and review your values together. On page 140 is a *Small Group Agreement* with the values we've found most useful in sustaining healthy, balanced groups. We recommend that you choose one or two values—ones you haven't previously focused on or have room to grow in—to emphasize during this study. Choose ones that will take your group to the next stage of intimacy and spiritual health.

-   If your group is new, welcome newcomers. Introduce everyone— you may even want to have nametags for your first meeting.

-   The *Small Group Calendar* on page 142 is a tool for planning who will host and lead each meeting. Take a few minutes to plan hosts and leaders for your remaining meetings. Don't skip this important step! It will revolutionize your group.

WATCH *now*

DVD SESSION ONE

Watch the DVD for this session now. Use the space provided below to record any key thoughts, questions, and things you want to remember or follow up on.

After watching the video, have someone read the discussion questions in the *Hear God's Story* section and direct the discussion among the group. As you go through each of the subsequent sections, ask someone else to read the next question and rotate who directs the discussion.

HEAR *God's* STORY

READ LUKE 23:33-34

When they came to the place called the Skull, they crucified Him there, along with the criminals—one on his right, the other on his left. Jesus said, "Father, forgive them, for they do not know what they are doing."

God uses stories to guide us. When we read the true stories of Scripture, we learn what God is like—we see His plan unfolding. And we learn principles for our own lives. How can we become a part of God's story? By aligning our stories with His. By not just understanding what it means to follow Him, but actually doing it—changing our attitudes and actions to live as He would live. Use the following questions to guide your discussion of the teaching and stories you just experienced, as well as the Bible passage to the left.

1. *What images or thoughts come to mind when you hear the verses above? What feelings do you have when you consider that the Son of God was crucified with criminals, although He had committed no crime? What else strikes you when you imagine this scene?

2. *In the teaching, Fr. Charlie called forgiveness "costly." Why was it so costly for God to forgive us?

3. In what ways does it feel costly to you when you forgive someone who has wronged you—whether it's a serious violation such as abuse or a smaller wrong such as being misunderstood? What are you having to let go of when you forgive another person?

4. Isn't it remarkable that Christ prayed these words of forgiveness as they were crucifying Him? In Romans 5:8 the Apostle Paul says, "But God demonstrates his own love for us in this: While we were still sinners, Christ died for us." How do you make sense of Jesus' prayer of forgiveness in the midst of persecution and violence? In what way does His petition include us as its object?

5. ...he people who witness ... Him, and mock ...sks God to ... else, how could ...ow His example

STUDY

NOTES

THE CRUCIFIED LIFE. In the teaching, Fr. Charlie said that we must deny self and follow Christ every day. Forgiveness is a "dying to self." Instead of insisting we are right or proving that someone else is wrong, we put our pride to death. What else do we "put to death" when we forgive someone who has wronged us?

ATONEMENT. Think of atonement as the "coinage" used to pay or satisfy completely the full cost of sin and violation. Jesus' death paid the price in full for our sins that we might be free from having to pay the debt ourselves. Jesus also paid the price in full for the sins of people who hurt you.

FREEDOM. Louis B. Smedes, whose book *Forgive and Forget: Healing the Hurts We Don't Deserve*, said "To forgive is to set a prisoner free and discover that the prisoner was you." Accepting Christ's forgiveness gives us true freedom from our sin.

ANGER. Forgiving others frees us from being imprisoned by bitterness, anger, and hatred. Thomas Chalmers is often quoted as saying "Unforgiveness is the poison we drink hoping another will die."

CREATE *a* NEW STORY

God wants you to be a part of His Kingdom, to weave your story into His. That will mean change—to go His way rather than your own. This won't happen overnight, but it should happen steadily. By starting with small, simple choices, we begin to change our direction. The Holy Spirit helps us along the way—giving us gifts to serve the body, offering us insights into Scripture, and challenging us to love not only those around us but those far from God.

In this section, talk about how you will apply the wisdom you've learned from the teaching and Bible study. Then think about practical steps you can take in the coming week to live out what you've learned.

7. In the teaching, Fr. Charlie says that when we pass the peace, we are testifying that we are "at peace with the Body of Christ." When have you experienced this in your life or seen it in the life of someone you know well? The next time you pass the peace, remember you are stating that you forgive and are at peace with Christ and His Church. Those whose hands you shake or whom you embrace are the sacrament of full membership in the body of Christ. How does that understanding change the way you look at the Peace?

8. Is there anyone with whom you do not feel at peace or for whom you have, as Fr. Charlie calls it, "unforgiveness"? If possible, speak to the person you feel has wronged you. If that person is deceased or if for another reason that isn't possible, ask God to help you forgive him or her. Begin to let go of resentment and the desire to change the past. Share your intentions with the group, if you feel comfortable doing so.

9. When you next pray the Lord's Prayer, focus on the words about forgiveness. "Forgive us our sins as we forgive those who sin against us" (Luke 11:4, NLT). Be honest with yourself: Is there someone you have been refusing to forgive? Can you talk about why it's so difficult for you?

To close your time together, spend some time worshiping God together—praying, singing, reading Scripture. The following are ways which you may consider closing your time together before the throne of God. Make it a time of praise and worship, as the words remind you of all God has done for you in Jesus Christ.

- You may have someone in your group with musical gifts. Consider inviting them to lead the group in a worship song. Try singing a song like *Amazing Grace* a cappella, use a worship CD, or have someone accompany your singing with a musical instrument. More than a dozen composers have put Christ's last words to music, including perhaps the most famous composition by Hayden. Consider sharing parts of this musical work over the next several weeks and simply meditating quietly and prayerfully allowing our Christian musical heritage to minister to your heart and soul.

- Choose a psalm or other favorite verse and read it aloud together, or pray the Lord's Prayer together.

- Ask "How can we pray for you this week?" Invite everyone to share, but don't force the issue. Be sure to write prayer requests on your *Prayer and Praise Report* on page 144

Close your meeting with prayer.

for ADDITIONAL STUDY

If you feel God nudging you to go deeper, take some time between now and our next meeting to dig into His word. Explore the Bible passages related to this session's theme on your own, jotting your reflections in a journal or in this study guide. A great way to gain insight on a passage is to read it in several different translations. You may want to use a Bible app or website to compare translations.

READ PSALM 103:1-11 (p. 733 in the *BCP*)

Bless the Lord, O my soul,
and all that is within me, bless His holy Name.
Bless the Lord, O my soul,
and forget not all His benefits.
He forgives all your sins
and heals all your infirmities;
He redeems your life from the grave
and crowns you with mercy and loving-kindness;
He satisfies you with good things,
and your youth is renewed like an eagle's.
The Lord executes righteousness
and judgment for all who are oppressed.
He made His ways known to Moses
and His works to the children of Israel.
The Lord is full of compassion and mercy,
slow to anger and of great kindness.
He will not always accuse us,
nor will He keep his anger forever.
He has not dealt with us according to our sins,
nor rewarded us according to our wickedness.
For as the heavens are high above the earth,
so is His mercy great upon those who fear him.

The Psalmist says that God is "full of compassion and mercy." In what ways have you witnessed God's mercy and kindness? In what ways do we reflect the image of God when we show compassion to others?

READ MICAH 7:18-19

Who is a God like you, who pardons sin and forgives the transgression of the remnant of his inheritance? You do not stay angry forever but delight to show mercy. You will again have compassion on us; you will tread our sins underfoot and hurl all our iniquities into the depths of the sea.

In these verses, God "hurls" our sins into the depths of the ocean. In other parts of the Scriptures, God says He will remember our sins "no more." That means that after He forgives us, He truly forgets our sins.

Is it hard to take God at His word and believe we are forgiven and our sins are forgotten? Do we ever continue to ruminate about what we've done wrong and how we have failed ourselves, others, or God? This week, what are ways to accept God's grace and reflect on God's promise to forgive and to forget our transgressions?

DAILY
DEVOTIONS

Remember to set aside time each day to read the Daily Devotion found in *The Crucified Life* book. These devotions will help you go deeper into this week's teaching. Listen to what God wants to say to you through His Word, and respond to Him as you meditate on the truths of Scripture.

There are seven Daily Devotions each week, except for this first week, in which there are four. The Devotions this week begin with Ash Wednesday and continue through the end of the week.

SALVATION

Truly, I say to you, today you will be with me in paradise.

If we confess our sins, He is faithful and just and will forgive us our sins and purify us from all unrighteousness.

1 JOHN 1:9

This week we reflect on the second of Christ's seven last "words," found in the Gospel of Luke (Luke 23:43).

Two criminals were crucified with Christ on the day we refer to as Good Friday. One of them shouted insults at Jesus, while the other recognized that Christ was blameless and did not deserve this terrible punishment.

This second man asks Jesus to "remember me," and Christ promises him that they will be together in paradise. The thief wants to be known by Christ; Christ promises reunion and relationship.

This week, we'll consider:

-        What is the difference between guilt and shame?
-        What does shame feel like?
-        How does Christ view our weaknesses?

Like the thief on the cross, we are invited to a restored relationship with God, one that is free of both guilt *and* shame. We'll explore what this relationship looks and feels like—together.

SHARE *your* STORY

As we said last week, when we tell our stories, sharing them with others, we give others the opportunity to see God at work. Your story is being shaped, even in this moment, by being a part of this group. In fact, few things can shape us more than community.

When we share our stories, we can encourage someone else, and learn. We can experience the presence of God as He helps us be brave enough to reveal our thoughts and feelings.

Open your group with prayer. This should be a brief, simple prayer, in which you invite God to guide you as you meet, to give you insight and wisdom. You can pray for specific requests at the end of the meeting, or stop momentarily to pray if a particular situation comes up during your discussion.

If you prefer, you could use this prayer from the Book of Common Prayer (p. 218):

Almighty God, whose blessed Son was led by the Spirit to be tempted by Satan; Come quickly to help us who are assaulted by many temptations; and, as you know the weaknesses of each of us, let each one find you mighty to save; through Jesus Christ your Son our Lord, who lives and reigns with you and the Holy Spirit, one God, now and forever. Amen.

Then, begin your time together by using the following questions and activities to get people talking.

1. *When you consider this part of the crucifixion story, which person do you identify with the most? The criminal who skeptically addresses Christ? The other convict, broken and humbled, who longs to be known by God? Or Jesus, wrongly accused and punished but yearning to extend love to others?

2. How does it strike you that Jesus, even while suffering on the cross, so quickly promises the criminal that they will be together in paradise? The man hasn't even confessed his sins, other than pointing out that "this man has done nothing wrong"—unlike himself—and doesn't deserve to die. Yet, Jesus immediately reassures and welcomes him.

EXTRA NOTE SPACE

....

....

....

....

....

....

....

....

....

....

....

WATCH *now*

DVD SESSION TWO

Watch the DVD for this session now. Use the *Notes* space provided here to record any key thoughts, questions, and things you want to remember or follow up on.

HEAR *God's* STORY

READ HEBREWS 12:1-3

Therefore, since we are surrounded by such a great cloud of witnesses, let us throw off everything that hinders and the sin that so easily entangles. And let us run with perseverance the race marked out for us, fixing our eyes on Jesus, the pioneer and perfecter of faith. For the joy set before Him He endured the cross, scorning its shame, and sat down at the right hand of the throne of God. Consider Him who endured such opposition from sinners, so that you will not grow weary and lose heart.

How can we become a part of God's story? When we align our stories with His, we gain greater understanding of what it means to follow Him. Use the following questions to guide your discussion of the teaching and stories you just experienced, and this Bible passage.

1. The writer of Hebrews differentiates between "everything that hinders" and "sin that entangles." Do you sometimes mistake your own personal weaknesses for sins? Explain.

2. *Identify any burdens you bear—disadvantages, faults, painful memories—that cause you to "lose heart" in your faith and daily life.

3. *Notice the use of the word "shame" in the passage above. Remember Christ's sacrifice paid for our guilt and restored an "unashamed" relationship with God. In Christ, we are not only forgiven, but also set free from feelings of failure, dread, and condemnation. What is one step you want to take toward freedom in this area?

STUDY

NOTES

GUILT. In his teaching, Fr. Charlie said that *guilt* is an appropriate response to breaking God's commandments. When I sin, I *feel* guilty—because I *am* guilty. Guilt is very specific, as it can be related to a specific sinful act which I committed.

SHAME. But *shame*, he explained, has to do with personhood: shame is related to the sense of defilement, failure, embarrassment and fear associated with sinful acts done *by* us or those of others done *to* us. Shame is a feeling of dread or condemnation. Shame makes us want to hide from God and others.

EMPATHY. But, in this second last word of Christ, we see Jesus reach out in love to the criminal who is dying beside Him. The man calls out to Jesus to be known and remembered by Jesus. With compassion and mercy, Christ quickly assures, restores and accepts him. Jesus bears our shame.

SALVATION. God's will for our lives is our salvation; He wants to restore relationship with us so that we might enjoy His presence, clothed in his grace and boldly unashamed.

CREATE *a* NEW STORY

In this section, talk about how you will apply the wisdom you've learned from the teaching and Bible study. Then think about practical steps you can take in the coming week to live out what you've learned.

4. When have you felt ashamed of yourself or others? Do you remember ever using the phrase, "Shame on you"? If so, describe the situation.

5. *Have you ever noticed that we have feelings of shame because of violations and abuses of our personhood by other people? Why would that be?

6. *In the video, Fr. Charlie encourages us to "internalize" God's forgiveness. What decisions have you made in the past for which you have lingering guilt or shame? Might you be ready now to let go of them and hold fast to the promise of salvation?

7. *Jesus "sympathizes with us in our weakness." Take a few moments to consider this. In what ways, over the course of your whole life, has Jesus Christ been sympathizing with you? Does anything prevent you from being vulnerable before Him?

8. When you speak the word "salvation," what does it mean to you? Did today's session cause you to understand that concept in a new way?

9. Take a look at the *Circles of Life* diagram on page 49 and write the names of two or three people you know who need to know Christ's salvation. Commit to praying for God's guidance and an opportunity to share with each of them. Share your lists with the group so that you can all be praying for the people you've identified.

10. Developing our ability to serve according to the leading of the Holy Spirit takes time and persistence in getting to know our Lord. So the first step toward serving others is, paradoxically, spending time alone with God: praying, studying, and reflecting on God's Word. Here are some simple ways to connect with God. Tell the group which one you plan to try this week, and then talk about your progress and challenges when you meet next time.

- **Prayer.** Commit to personal prayer and daily connection with God. You may find it helpful to write your prayers in a journal.

- **Daily Devotions.** The Daily Devotions provided in *The Crucified Life* book offer an opportunity to read a short Bible passage five days a week during the course of this study. In our hurry-up world, we often move too quickly through everything—even reading God's Word! Slow down. Don't just skim, but take time to read carefully and reflect on the passage. Write down your insights on what you read each day. Copy a portion of Scripture on a card and tape it somewhere in your line of sight, such as your car's dashboard or the bathroom mirror. Or text it to yourself! Think about it when you sit at red lights, or while you're eating a meal. Reflect on what God is saying to you through these words. On the sixth day summarize what God has shown you throughout the week.

11. To close your time, spend some time worshiping God together—praying, singing, reading Scripture.

- Have someone use their musical gifts to lead the group in a worship song. Try singing a cappella, using a worship CD, or have someone accompany your singing with a musical instrument. If you are using Hayden's or another of the musical compositions to which Christ's last words are set, play that now.

- Choose a psalm or other favorite verse and read it aloud together. Make it a time of praise and worship, as the words remind you of all that God has done for you.

- Ask "How can we pray for you this week?" Invite everyone to share, but don't force the issue. Be sure to write prayer requests on your *Prayer and Praise Report* on page 144.

- Close your meeting with prayer.

for ADDITIONAL STUDY

If you feel God nudging you to go deeper, take some time between now and our next meeting to dig into His Word. Explore the Bible passages below on your own, jotting your reflections in a journal or in this study guide. Want to go deeper? Select a few verses and try paraphrasing them—writing them in your own words. If you like, share them with the group the next time you meet.

READ JOHN 15:9-13

As the Father has loved me, so have I loved you. Now remain in my love. If you keep my commands, you will remain in my love, just as I have kept my Father's commands and remain in his love. I have told you this so that my joy may be in you and that your joy may be complete. My command is this: Love each other as I have loved you. Greater love has no one than this: to lay down one's life for one's friends.

What is your gut reaction to the idea that Christ takes pleasure in knowing you?

What are some ways you can "remain" in God's love? A few ideas include receiving the Eucharist and studying the Bible with others. What other ways can you think of?

Reflect on the idea that Christ said He loves us *as God loved Him.* What might that love feel like? Can you think of ways God has shown His love for you?

READ ISAIAH 50:7

Because the Sovereign Lord helps me,
I will not be disgraced.
Therefore have I set my face like flint,
and I know I will not be put to shame.

What comes to mind when you imagine a face that is "set…like flint"? A person with such an expression would appear to be undaunted, resolute and determined.

Throughout the Scriptures, we are told again and again that God is on our side and will help us. Many scholars say that some form of the phrase "Do not be afraid" is repeated at least 365 times in the Bible. This verse reminds us that God's will for us is salvation, grace and peace, not disgrace or shame.

Thank God for His love and protection, and approach Him with confidence.

DAILY
DEVOTIONS

Use the Daily Devotions in *The Crucified Life* book to further explore this week's topic. Read the devotional reflection each day and take time to think through the questions at the end. Ask God to speak to you through His Word and to transform your life by His love and mercy.

RELATIONSHIP

Woman, behold your son... Behold your mother.

So you are no longer a slave, but God's child; and since you are his child, God has made you also an heir.

GALATIANS 4:7

Jesus addressed the third of His last words from the cross to His mother—Mary, and John—Jesus' disciple and cherished friend. Many people had already left the scene of the crucifixion, but these two intimates of Christ remained with Him to the end.

Even as He sacrifices Himself for the redemption of humankind, Jesus remembers and honors His role as Mary's son. He asks John to care for her when, from the cross, He names them as family. *Woman, behold your son. John, behold your mother.*

In this week's session, we'll explore the concept of *family* and the blessings—and challenges—it can deliver. We'll learn how, in Christ, we are welcomed into a *new* family, a spiritual one, established by God.

SHARE *your* STORY

Open your group with prayer. This should be a brief, simple prayer, in which you invite God to be with you as you meet. You can pray for specific requests at the end of the meeting, or stop momentarily to pray if a particular situation comes up during your discussion.

You could also pray this Collect from the Book of Common Prayer (BCP, p. 124)

O God and Father of all, whom the whole heavens adore: Let the whole earth also worship you, all nations obey you, all tongues confess and bless you, and men and women everywhere love you and serve you in peace; through Jesus Christ our Lord. Amen.

Telling our personal stories builds deeper connections among group members. Begin your time together by using the following questions and activities to get people talking.

Last week we talked about what it means to be freed from guilt and shame by the one who is "mighty to save"—Jesus Christ. This week, we'll look at what it means to be members of God's family together.

1. When you hear the word "family," what descriptors come to mind? Why do you think families sometimes have trouble getting along?

2. What does it mean to you to be in the household of God?

EXTRA NOTE SPACE

....

....

....

....

....

....

....

....

....

....

....

....

....

....

....

WATCH *now*

DVD SESSION THREE

Watch the DVD for this session now. Use the *Notes* space provided here to record any key thoughts, questions, and things you want to remember or follow up on.

HEAR *God's* STORY

READ MATTHEW 12:46-50

While Jesus was still talking to the crowd, his mother and brothers stood outside, wanting to speak to him. Someone told him, "Your mother and brothers are standing outside, wanting to speak to you."

Use the following questions to guide your discussion of the teaching and Bible stories you just experienced on the DVD, and the Bible passage on the left.

He replied to him, "Who is my mother, and who are my brothers?" Pointing to his disciples, he said, "Here are my mother and my brothers. For whoever does the will of my Father in heaven is my brother and sister and mother."

1.   *What surprises you about Jesus' statement? In what ways do these words seem out of character or even unloving?

2.   What are a few different ways we can interpret these words? Was Jesus rejecting His family? What else could He have been trying to communicate to those who were listening?

3.   How would you describe or define "the will of God"?

STUDY

NOTES

HUMAN FAMILIES. Ideally, our human families are loving, accepting and faithful to Christ. Too often, however, members of families hurt each other. Some children are abused. Some couples live in bitter acrimony. Some siblings compete and work against each other. Human families, as Fr. Charlie pointed out in the teaching, have been broken and dysfunctional since Adam and Eve.

GOD'S FAMILY. As we learned in the DVD, the Bible is the story of the broken human family and of God establishing a new family in Christ. As Christ looks down on His family (Mary and John), He sees another kind of family standing there also—rebellious soldiers who do not seek a relationship with Him. But, as Fr. Charlie said, Christ looks at the soldiers with love, longing for a restored relationship with them. We are invited into the household of God, regardless of how bitter, dysfunctional or far we are from Christ.

CREATE *a* NEW STORY

God wants you to be a part of His Kingdom—to weave your story into His. That will mean change. It will require you to go His way rather than your own. This won't happen overnight, but it should happen steadily. By making small, simple choices, we can begin to change our direction. The Holy Spirit helps us along the way, by giving us gifts to serve the body, offering us insights into Scripture, and challenging us to love not only those around us but those far from God.

In this section, talk about how you will apply the wisdom you've learned in this session.

4. *On the DVD, Fr. Charlie recommended that we look at our own family trees and discern generational patterns of sin. You may want to complete this exercise in your journal over the next several days or talk now about some of the unhealthy patterns you are aware of in your family of origin. How does the idea of doing this make you feel? Use the Family Tree exercise in the appendix (page 147) to guide your reflection.

5. *What do you most long for in your natural family relationships? How about your church family?

6. What specific steps will you take this week to cultivate your personal relationship with God? If you've focused on prayer in past weeks, maybe you'll want to direct your attention to Scripture this week. If you've been reading God's Word consistently, perhaps

you'll want to take it deeper and try memorizing a verse. Tell the group which one you plan to try this week, and then, at your next meeting, talk about your progress and challenges.

7. In the last session we asked you to write some names in the *Circles of Life* diagram. Who did you identify as the people in your life who need to meet Jesus? Go back to the *Circles of Life* diagram on page 49 to help you think of the various people you come in

contact with on a regular basis, people who need to know Jesus more deeply. Consider the following ideas for action and make a plan to follow through on one of them this week.

-   This is a wonderful time to welcome a few friends into your group. Which of the people you listed could you invite? It's possible that you may need to help your friend overcome obstacles to coming to a place where he or she can encounter Jesus. Does your friend need a ride to the group? Help with childcare?

-   Consider inviting a friend to attend a weekend service with you and possibly plan to enjoy a meal together afterward. This can be a great opportunity to talk with someone about your faith in Jesus.

-   Is there someone whom you wouldn't invite to your group but who still needs a connection? Would you be willing to have lunch or coffee with that person, catch up on life, and share something you've learned from this study? Jesus doesn't call all of us to lead small groups, but He does call every disciple to spiritually multiply his or her life over time.

-   Groups that connect outside of the regular meeting time build stronger bonds and feel a greater sense of purpose. Why not plan a social outing with group members? As a group, brainstorm about ways that you could do something fun together—enjoy a meal or a night out together?

8. To close your time together, spend some time worshiping God together—praying, singing, reading Scripture, as you've done in previous weeks.

-   Close your meeting with prayer. Be sure to write prayer requests on your *Prayer and Praise Report* on page 144.

for ADDITIONAL STUDY

Take some time between now and our next meeting to dig into God's Word. Explore the Bible passage below on your own, jotting your reflections in a journal or in this study guide. You may even want to use a Bible website or app to look up commentary on these passages. If you like, share what you learn with the group the next time you meet.

READ JOSHUA 24:15

But if serving the Lord seems undesirable to you, then choose for yourselves this day whom you will serve, whether the gods your ancestors served beyond the Euphrates, or the gods of the Amorites, in whose land you are living. But as for me and my household, we will serve the Lord.

How could patterns of generational sin, such as the ones Fr. Charlie discussed in his teaching (racism, addiction, greed) be likened to worshiping the "gods your ancestors served"?

In what ways do you and your household identify as a new, re-established family of God?

What characterizes a family who serves God?

READ EPHESIANS 2:13-19

But now in Christ Jesus you who once were far away have been brought near by the blood of Christ. For he himself is our peace, who has made the two groups one and has destroyed the barrier, the dividing wall of hostility, by setting aside in his flesh the law with its commands and regulations. His purpose was to create in himself one new humanity out of the two, thus making peace, and in one body to reconcile both of them to God through the cross, by which he put to death their hostility. He came and preached peace to you who were far away and peace to those who were near. For through him we both have access to the Father by one Spirit. Consequently, you are no longer foreigners and strangers, but fellow citizens with God's people and also members of his household.

The word "hostility" is repeated in these verses. When have you witnessed hostility in yourself or others? How might Christ bring peace to hostile situations? How can you be an instrument of such peace?

Think about a time you have traveled or otherwise been in a situation in which you were a "foreigner" or "stranger"? How did that feel? How can you echo Christ's love and welcome a stranger in your community?

What does it mean to you to belong to the "family of God"? Are you comfortable when someone says you are a brother or sister in Christ? What does that mean to you?

DAILY
DEVOTIONS

As you've done in previous weeks, read each day's Daily Devotion in *The Crucified Life* companion book. Hopefully, this devotional time is becoming a regular part of your day. God promises to be present with us as we take time to pray and study His word. This week, why not pray before your devotional time, asking God to lead you and guide your thoughts as you reflect on the teaching?

SESSION FOUR

DISTRESS

I thirst.

Whoever drinks the water I give them will never thirst. Indeed, the water I give them will become in them a spring of water welling up to eternal life.

JOHN 4:14

In this session, we look at Christ's shortest exclamation from the cross: "I thirst."

This statement can serve as a reminder that Christ was truly human and was subject to the same physical needs that we are; He knew hunger, He sometimes found Himself short of breath, and He experienced pain. Jesus had been through terrible physical suffering on the day of His crucifixion, and, after hanging on the cross for hours, He longed for something to drink.

But the word "thirst" can also be understood figuratively. This week we will consider what it is we "thirst for," as together we look at two different types of desires—desires of the flesh and desires of the Spirit.

SHARE *your* STORY

Open your group with prayer. This should be a brief, simple prayer, in which you invite God to be with you as you meet. You can pray for specific requests at the end of the meeting, or stop momentarily to pray if a particular situation comes up during your discussion.

Telling our personal stories builds deeper connections among group members. Begin your time together by using the following questions and activities to get people talking.

1. Think of a time when you were thirsty—either physically, spiritually, or emotionally? How was that thirst quenched?

2. *When you hear the question, "What do you thirst for?" what words or images immediately come to mind? A cold glass of ice water after working in the garden? A cola with your burger and fries? Or, do you thirst for something less tangible, such as healing, love or acceptance?

EXTRA NOTE SPACE

WATCH *now*

DVD SESSION FOUR

Watch the DVD for this session now. Use the *Notes* space provided here to record any key thoughts, questions, and things you want to remember or follow up on.

HEAR *God's* STORY

READ JOHN 7:37-38

On the last and greatest day of the festival, Jesus stood and said in a loud voice, "Let anyone who is thirsty come to me and drink. Whoever believes in me, as Scripture has said, rivers of living water will flow from within them."

Use the following questions to guide your discussion of the teaching and stories you just experienced on the DVD and the Bible passage to the left.

1. *What do you most thirst for? How have your cravings, desires, and thirsts evolved over the years as you mature and grow in Christ? What habits or desires have you seen Christ transform in your life or in the lives of those you love?

2. What types of water, in nature, would you describe as "living water"? When have you seen "living water" in a natural environment? What did it look like? Sound like? Feel like? Did you taste it? What was it like? What does Jesus mean when he offers us "living water"?

3. *At Communion, Christ gives us something to drink. What does it mean to you to receive the Eucharistic wine and bread—Christ's body and blood? When are other times your spiritual thirst has been addressed or satisfied?

4. What do you think it means when Jesus says, "rivers of living water will flow from within them"?

NOTES

DESIRES OF THE FLESH. During the past few weeks, we have considered what it means to live a "crucified" life, or to be dead to our sinful nature and alive in Christ. When we follow our "old nature" and sinful desires, we're drawn to destructive, fleshly desires and attitudes. Our sinful nature is jealous, impure and given to fits of anger. As we continue to die to self and follow Christ, the wounds and divisions that our old nature engenders will be replaced by abundant, grace-giving life.

DESIRES OF THE SPIRIT. When we are closely aligning our desires with Christ's, the "fruit" of the Spirit (Galatians 5:22-23) will come splashing and overflowing out of us, like living water. The fruit of the spirit is love, joy, peace, forbearance, kindness, goodness, faithfulness, gentleness and self-control.

What are the differences between desires of the flesh and desires of the Spirit? Contrast the two. Is it possible to have both desires at the same time? Why is it so hard to deny our flesh and satisfy the desires of the Spirit?

CREATE *a* NEW STORY

God wants you to be a part of His Kingdom—to weave your story into His. That will mean change—to go His way rather than your own. This won't happen overnight, but it should happen steadily. By starting with small, simple choices, we begin to change our direction. The Holy Spirit helps us along the way—giving us gifts to serve the body, offering us insights into Scripture, and challenging us to love not only those around us but those far from God.

In this section, talk about how you will apply the wisdom you've learned in this session.

5. *Fr. Charlie suggested making a "drink offering" or "free will offering" to Christ as we endeavor to die to self and express our love and gratitude to God. Lent is the traditional season in which we practice self-denial in order to make an offering of our lives to God. How has Lenten fasting, study or prayer affected your spiritual life?

6. Paul writes to Timothy (2 Tim. 4:6), "I am already being poured out like a drink offering, and the time for my departure is near." While Paul was speaking of his pending martyrdom for the faith, what are some practical ways to offer yourself as a "drink offering" to God?

7. *In what ways would you like to "spill over" with Christ's living water? Think about your daily life and the people with whom you have contact. How might you sprinkle them with the reviving fruit of the Spirit when you interact with them this week?

8. Each of you in the group has different gifts and abilities. And every small group has tasks and roles that need to be done. How could you serve this group—perhaps with hospitality, prayer, organizing an event, researching or studying a topic, worshiping or inviting new people? Have each person share what their gift or passion is and how they could use it to strengthen and build up the group.

9. Spend some time praying about those you know who might respond to a simple invitation— to come to a church service, to join your small group, or even to just have coffee and talk about spiritual matters. Ask the Holy Spirit to bring to mind people you can pray for.

10. *Groups grow closer when they serve together. How could you as a group serve someone in need? You may want to visit a shut-in from your church, provide a meal for a family going through difficulty, or give some other practical help to someone in need. If nothing comes to mind, spend some time as a group praying and asking God to show you who needs your help. Have two or three group members organize a serving project for the group, and then—do it!

for ADDITIONAL STUDY

Take some time between now and our next meeting to dig into God's Word. Explore the Bible passages related to this session's theme on your own, jotting your reflections in a journal or in this study guide. You may even want to use a Bible website or app to look up commentary on these passages. If you like, share what you learn with the group the next time you meet.

READ MATTHEW 25:35

For I was hungry and you gave me something to eat, I was thirsty and you gave me something to drink, I was a stranger and you invited me in…

In the book of Matthew, we learn that when we offer love, comfort or friendship to others, we are actually giving these things to Christ. Think about the people who "thirst" (whether physically or otherwise) in your community. How can you help to meet their needs? What are some ways your small group might create a "drink offering" and collaborate to provide food for the hungry or to make a stranger feel welcome and accepted?

READ ISAIAH 40:31

…but those who hope in the Lord
will renew their strength.
They will soar on wings like eagles;
they will run and not grow weary,
they will walk and not be faint.

Think about a time in your life when you have felt weary, when moving through the events of your life felt like a struggle? Have you ever felt a lack of hope?

In what ways have you or others whom you know "hoped in the Lord"?

When we hope in the Lord, we, too, experience freedom and can see our lives from a different angle. How would it feel to you if you were soaring on eagle's wings?

DAILY
DEVOTIONS

The Daily Devotions for this week, found in *The Crucified Life* companion book will further explore the fourth word of Christ from the cross: *I thirst.* You will discover that these two small words contain a volume of meaning in relation to Jesus' physical and spiritual distress on our behalf. The Daily Devotions are a wonderful way of keeping the spirit of Lent alive in your heart all through the week.

ABANDONMENT

My God, My God, why have you forsaken me?

Hear my prayer, Lord; listen to my cry for mercy.

PSALM 86:6

This week we look at Christ's fifth word from the cross—His cry of pain and abandonment.

Every one of us goes through difficult times of anguish and pain—times so excruciating that they cause us to question God's presence and goodness. Scholars often refer to these as "dark nights of the soul."

The problem of evil has been puzzled over for millennia.

How can we reconcile a belief in a loving God with the suffering we endure in this broken, difficult world?

Why do bad things happen to good people?

Why does God not intervene to save us from financial or emotional problems and sickness?

We will explore these kinds of questions this week, and we will also reflect on the most loving ways we can walk alongside someone who is plodding through a dark night of the soul.

SHARE *your* STORY

Open your group with prayer. This should be a brief, simple prayer, in which you invite God to be with you as you meet. You can pray for specific requests at the end of the meeting, or stop momentarily to pray if a particular situation comes up during your discussion.

Telling our personal stories builds deeper connections among group members. Begin your time together by using the following questions and activities to get people talking. Sharing our stories requires us to be honest. We can help one another to be honest and open by creating a safe place: be sure that your group is one where confidentiality is respected, where there's no such thing as "stupid questions," where you listen without criticizing one another.

1. *Why do people question the existence of God during difficult times?

2. Have you ever felt like God isn't hearing or responding to even your most desperate and heartfelt prayers?

3. Tell about a time you felt abandoned by people or by God. What happened? How did you get through it?

EXTRA NOTE SPACE

WATCH *now*

DVD SESSION FIVE

Watch the DVD for this session now. Use the *Notes* space provided here to record any key thoughts, questions, and things you want to remember or follow up on.

HEAR *God's* STORY

READ 2 CHRONICLES

6:14

Lord, the God of Israel, there is no God like you in heaven or on earth—you who keep your covenant of love with your servants who continue wholeheartedly in your way.

Use the following questions to guide your discussion of the teaching from the DVD and the Bible passage here.

1. Does this verse, beautiful as it is, seem to push against the content of this week's lesson? That is, how is God keeping "a covenant of love" with His people when He allows them to suffer?

2. *Do verses like this ever cause you to wonder whether you really do know God? If you are His servant, yet you find yourself in crisis, do you ever doubt your faith and/or God's love?

3. Does it feel natural or comfortable to lament or question God's goodness? *Have you ever prayed or thought the words, "Why has God forsaken me?" Can you describe how that felt and what kept you trusting in Christ even after experiencing such despair?

NOTES

LAMENT. To "lament" means to express sorrow, grief or regret. When we lament, we deeply mourn. Many of the Psalms are considered "Psalms of Lament." These emotionally charged expressions do not gloss over the pain the Psalmist experiences but instead are raw, honest expressions of question, fear, abandonment or betrayal. Laments can make other people feel *uncomfortable*.

PLATITUDES. Platitudes are "flat" statements of response to suffering that are usually offered to end meaningful conversation rather than to open it. They may make the one offering the platitude feel better—but never the receiver. In his teaching, Fr. Charlie encourages us to avoid platitudes and grieve with those who grieve.

REFLECTIVE LISTENING. He described his practice of "reflective listening" and encouraged us to allow others to reflect and vent authentically with us when they are suffering. Reflective listening repeats back emotion and content to the one suffering. It can be phrased in a simple way such as, "You feel _____ because of _____." When we truly empathize with others—or when others empathize with us—we are lifted up from our despair.

CREATE *a* NEW STORY

God wants you to be a part of His Kingdom—to weave your story into His. That will mean change. It will require you to go His way rather than your own. This won't happen overnight, but it should happen steadily. By making small, simple choices, we can begin to change our direction. The Holy Spirit helps us along the way, by giving us gifts to serve the body, offering us insights into Scripture, and challenging us to love not only those around us but those far from God.

In this section, talk about how you will apply the wisdom you've learned in this session.

4. *What platitudes have you spoken—or had someone say to you—in difficult times? What specific words have been most and least helpful to you when you've felt lonely, disappointed or grieving?

5. Have you ever been in a situation, similar to the one Fr. Charlie described from his days as a chaplain, where someone seemed at the very end of him- or herself? How do you feel when faced with such raw pain? What did you say or do in that moment?

6. *What did Father Charlie mean by "reflective listening"? In what situation would you be able to apply that skill?

7. Spend some time praying about those you know who might respond to a simple invitation—to come to a church service, to join your small group, or even to just have coffee and talk about spiritual matters. Ask the Holy Spirit to bring to mind people you can pray for.

8. *A strong group is made up of people who are all being filled up by God, so that they are empowered to love one another. What specific steps will you take this week to connect with God privately so that He can "fill you up"? If you've focused on prayer in past weeks, maybe you'll want to direct your attention to Scripture this week. If you've been reading God's Word consistently, perhaps you'll want to take it deeper and try memorizing a verse. Tell the group which one you plan to try this week, and then, at your next meeting, talk about your progress and challenges.

9. To close your time, spend some time worshiping God together—praying, singing, reading Scripture.

- Have someone use their musical gifts to lead the group in a worship song. Try singing a cappella, using a worship CD, or having someone accompany your singing with a musical instrument.

- Read a passage of Scripture together, making it a time of praise and worship as the words remind you of all God has done for you. Choose a psalm or other favorite verse.

- Ask everyone to share: "How can we pray for you this week?" Be sure to write prayer requests on your *Prayer and Praise Report* on page 144.

- Close your meeting with prayer. This week, you may wish to use this prayer from the *Book of Common Prayer* (*BCP*, p. 134).

Keep watch, dear Lord, with those who work, or watch, or weep this night, and give your angels charge over those who sleep. Tend the sick, Lord Christ; give rest to the weary, bless the dying, soothe the suffering, pity the afflicted, shield the joyous; and all for your love's sake. Amen.

EXTRA NOTE SPACE

for ADDITIONAL STUDY

Take some time between now and our next meeting to dig into God's Word. Explore the Bible passages related to this session's theme on your own, jotting your reflections in a journal or in this study guide. You may even want to use a Bible website or app to look up commentary on these passages. If you like, share what you learn with the group the next time you meet.

READ PSALM 88:1-5, 12-14

Lord, you are the God who saves me;
day and night I cry out to you.
May my prayer come before you;
turn your ear to my cry.
I am overwhelmed with troubles
and my life draws near to death.
I am counted among those who go down to the pit;
I am like one without strength.
I am set apart with the dead,
like the slain who lie in the grave,
whom you remember no more,
who are cut off from your care.
...
Are your wonders known in the place of darkness,
or your righteous deeds in the land of oblivion?
But I cry to you for help, Lord;
in the morning my prayer comes before you.
Why, Lord, do you reject me
and hide your face from me?

The Psalmist cries out words that are echoed in Christ's fifth word from the cross: "Why, Lord, do you hide your face from me?" What goes through your mind and heart when you feel rejected, especially by God? If you have been through an injustice, does this Psalm vocalize your heart's cry? How would you express it? How do you wrestle with the problem of evil in prayer?

READ LUKE 12:22-34

Then Jesus said to his disciples: "Therefore I tell you, do not worry about your life, what you will eat; or about your body, what you will wear. For life is more than food, and the body more than clothes. Consider the ravens: They do not sow or reap, they have no storeroom or barn; yet God feeds them. And how much more valuable you are than birds! Who of you by worrying can add a single hour to your life? Since you cannot do this very little thing, why do you worry about the rest? Consider how the wild flowers grow. They do not labor or spin. Yet I tell you, not even Solomon in all his splendor was dressed like one of these. If that is how God clothes the grass of the field, which is here today, and tomorrow is thrown into the fire, how much more will he clothe you—you of little faith! And do not set your heart on what you will eat or drink; do not worry about it. For the pagan world runs after all such things, and your Father knows that you need them. But seek his kingdom, and these things will be given to you as well. Do not be afraid, little flock, for your Father has been pleased to give you the kingdom. Sell your possessions and give to the poor. Provide purses for yourselves that will not wear out, a treasure in heaven that will never fail, where no thief comes near and no moth destroys. For where your treasure is, there your heart will be also."

Remembering last week's discussion of two types of "thirst" (thirsting for God versus craving earthly things), in what ways can our suffering be affected by—or even caused by—our sinful desires? That is, do we ever feel disappointment, resentment or regret because we are seeking after the wrong things?

DAILY
DEVOTIONS

As you've done in previous weeks, be sure to set aside time each day for the Daily Devotions found in *The Crucified Life* book. These in-depth reflections will help you stay connected to Christ throughout the week and the entire season of Lent. After the reading, take some time to reflect to Him in prayer or in a journal about your personal response to the truths of the Scriptures.

SESSION SIX

REUNION

Father, into your hands I commend my Spirit.

But I trust in you, Lord; I say, "You are my God."

PSALM 31:14

In this second to last of Christ's final words, Jesus expresses anticipation that the Father will receive Him. He anticipates reunion with the Father despite the agony and sense of abandonment He has experienced.

This week we will explore how we can trust God in the most painful moments of our life, especially when we are treated unjustly. When Christ commends His spirit to the Father, He models for us the way to navigate difficult times—we are to trust in God's steadfast love.

We'll explore questions such as:

- How do we "bear up" when we are being treated wrongly?
- What are different ways to understand the word "trust"?
- What is Christ's example of trust for us?

Together, in this session, we will look at ways we can more fully trust God.

SHARE *your* STORY

Open your group with prayer. This should be a brief, simple prayer, in which you invite God to be with you as you meet. You can pray for specific requests at the end of the meeting, or stop momentarily to pray if a particular situation comes up during your discussion.

You may wish to use this Collect from the Book of Common Prayer (BCP, p. 218):

Almighty and everliving God, in your tender love for the human race you sent your Son our Savior Jesus Christ to take upon him our nature, and to suffer death upon the cross, giving us the example of his great humility: Mercifully grant that we may walk in the way of his suffering, and also share in his resurrection; through Jesus Christ our Lord, who lives and reigns with you and the Holy Spirit, one God, for ever and ever. Amen.

Telling our personal stories builds deeper connections among group members. Begin your time together by using the following questions and activities to get people talking. Sharing our stories requires us to be honest. We can help one another to be honest and open by creating a safe place: be sure that your group is one where confidentiality is respected, where there is no such thing as a "stupid question," where you listen without criticizing one another.

1. Why do some people have a hard time trusting God or other people?

2. What happens to a person when his or her trust is shattered?

EXTRA NOTE SPACE

WATCH *now*

DVD SESSION SIX

Watch the DVD for this session now. Use the Notes space provided here to record any key thoughts, questions, and things you want to remember or follow up on.

HEAR *God's* STORY

READ PSALM 31:17-24

Let me not be put to shame, Lord, for I have cried out to you; but let the wicked be put to shame and be silent in the realm of the dead. Let their lying lips be silenced, for with pride and contempt they speak arrogantly against the righteous. How abundant are the good things that you have stored up for those who fear you, that you bestow in the sight of all, on those who take refuge in you. In the shelter of your presence you hide them from all human intrigues; you keep them safe in your dwelling from accusing tongues. Praise be to the Lord, for he showed me the wonders of his love when I was in a city under siege. In my alarm I said, "I am cut off from your sight!" Yet you heard my cry for mercy when I called to you for help. Love the Lord, all his faithful people! The Lord preserves those who are true to him, but the proud he pays back in full. Be strong and take heart, all you who hope in the Lord.

Use the following questions to guide your discussion of the teaching from the DVD and the Bible passage below.

1. At the beginning of the passage above, the Psalmist asks that he not be put to shame, but that those who treat him wrongly would be shamed. The writer of this Psalm begs that he not feel ashamed or, as Fr. Charlie put it a few weeks ago, unworthy or full of dread. Are you burdened by any unkind and untrue things that have been said about you? Can you release these to Jesus, and ask that He fill you with joy and wonder in His love?

2. *In this passage, the Psalmist describes himself as a "city under siege." Tell about a time you felt like you were being personally, professionally, or spiritually attacked from all sides? How did you respond?

3. What promise does this Psalm give regarding those who unjustly accuse us? How does it instruct us to pray for our persecutors?

4. *Note how this Psalm ends. The Psalmist has come to a moment of resolution and peace when he asserts that God is caring and just. Looking back on some of the most difficult moments in your life, do you discern how God preserved you or even silenced the tongues of those who gossiped about you?

STUDY

NOTES

UNJUST SUFFERING. The Bible is filled with examples of men and women of God who suffer unjustly as they live faithfully in this fallen and sinful world. Jesus is the supreme example of an innocent who suffers unjustly.

TRUST. Moments of unjust suffering require a special faith to believe God is good and sovereign, even though we may not see the big picture or understand why.

HESED. Hesed is the Hebrew word for God's steadfast love and covenant faithfulness. Jesus commended Himself to the hand of the Father knowing that His Father loved Him and is absolutely trustworthy in His will. The Apostle Paul promises in Romans that even though we will suffer in this age, there is nothing in all of creation that can "separate us from the love of God that is in Christ Jesus our Lord" (Romans 8:36-39).

CREATE *a* NEW STORY

God wants you to be a part of His Kingdom—to weave your story into His. That will mean change—to go His way rather than your own. This won't happen overnight, but it should happen steadily. By starting with small, simple choices, we begin to change our direction. The Holy Spirit helps us along the way—giving us gifts to serve the body, offering us insights into Scripture, and challenging us to love not only those around us but those far from God.

In this section, talk about how you will apply the wisdom you've learned in this session.

5.   As we know, and as even the criminal who was suffering and dying beside Jesus could see, Christ's torment and crucifixion was not deserved. He was blameless, yet He was unjustly put to death. When you are unjustly treated, how do typically respond? What keeps you from forgiving those who hurt you? How could you follow Jesus' model?

6.   *Fr. Charlie highlighted the Hebrew word *hesed* in his teaching this week. Used more than 240 times in the Old Testament, *hesed* describes God's steadfast love. What's one situation in your life where you long to experience the *hesed* of God?

7. *As this is the second to last meeting in this study, take some time to celebrate the work God has done in the lives of group members. Have each person in the group share some step of growth that they have noticed in *another* member. (In other words, no one will talk about himself or herself. Instead, affirm others in the group.) Make sure that each person gets affirmed and noticed and celebrated, whether the steps they've made are large or small.

8. A strong group is made up of people who are all being filled with the love of God, so that they are empowered to love one another. What specific steps will you take this week to connect with God privately, so that He can fill you with His love? If you've focused on prayer in past weeks, maybe you'll want to direct your attention to Scripture this week. If you've been reading God's Word consistently, perhaps you'll want to take it deeper and try memorizing a verse. Tell the group which one you plan to try this week, and then, at your next meeting, talk about your progress and challenges.

9. *Discuss the upcoming Holy Week services. The Palm Sunday, Maundy Thursday, and Good Friday liturgies are climactic Holy Moments for which this Lenten season has been preparing you. As a group, make a commitment to attend together as many of these services as you are able. Also discuss when you will meet again for the last session on Triumph so that your group meeting time is not in conflict with your Holy Week worship. Take the things that have been stirred in you by the Seven Last Words of Jesus to the foot of the Cross.

10. Ask everyone to share: "How can we pray for you this week?" Be sure to write prayer requests on your *Prayer and Praise Report* on page 144. Close your meeting with prayer.

for ADDITIONAL STUDY

Take some time between now and our next meeting to dig into God's Word. Explore the Bible passages related to this session's theme on your own, jotting your reflections in a journal or in this study guide. You may even want to use a Bible website or app to look up commentary on these passages. If you like, share what you learn with the group the next time you meet.

READ PSALM 51:7

Cleanse me with hyssop, and I will be clean; wash me, and I will be whiter than snow.

Every Sunday during the Eucharist, the priest prays,

Almighty God, to you all hearts are open, all desires known, and from you no secrets are hid: Cleanse the thoughts of our hearts by the inspiration of your Holy Spirit, that we may perfectly love you, and worthily magnify your holy Name; through Christ our Lord. Amen (BCP, p. 355).

When we are out of the habit of trusting, or when our minds are cluttered with worry, we can ask God to *cleanse our thoughts* so that we may approach God the Father like the beloved, trusting children we are. What specific fears, anxieties or memories could you lay at the altar as you open your heart and trust God more fully?

READ ROMANS 15:13

May the God of hope fill you with all joy and peace as you trust in him, so that you may overflow with hope by the power of the Holy Spirit.

The more we trust in God, the more secure we feel in our faith, regardless of the painful or disappointing times we have experienced.

Do the words "overflowing with hope" in the verse above remind you of that living water Jesus describes? Have you ever experienced a sloshing-over of the hope, joy and love you have within you? St. Paul's joyful and hope-filled blessing, recorded in the book of Romans is offered to us today. Read that verse again and imagine it is being spoken directly to you. Perhaps insert your name into it:

May the God of hope fill you, _____, with all joy and peace as you trust in Him.

DAILY
DEVOTIONS

This week, the Daily Devotions in *The Crucified Life* book will help you further explore the sixth word spoken by Jesus from the cross: "Father, into your hands I commend my spirit." Like a multi-faceted diamond, the Daily Devotions uncover the many sides of the text and allow you to experience the light of God's truth from many vantage points. Be sure to take time each day for these devotional reflections.

SESSION SEVEN

TRIUMPH

It is finished.

Each of you should use whatever gift you have received to serve others, as faithful stewards of God's grace in its various forms.

1 PETER 4:10

This week, as we complete our study of *The Crucified Life*, we will consider the seventh and final utterance Christ made from the cross.

This pronouncement, "It is finished," is much more than a dying man's last words. It announces to the Father that Jesus has accomplished what He was sent to do. Christ has persevered through the agony of the crucifixion, and His work is complete.

This week we will delve into the idea of *calling* and explore what God has given for each of us to do, both *personally* and *corporately* as people of faith.

We'll discuss several aspects of calling, and we will be encouraged to persevere, no matter how close or far we are from completing what God has asked us to do. We'll be reminded that each one of us has been called by God in the work of bringing about His kingdom.

SHARE *your* STORY

Open your group with prayer. This should be a brief, simple prayer, in which you invite God to be with you as you meet. You can pray for specific requests at the end of the meeting or stop momentarily to pray if a particular situation comes up during your discussion.

You could also use this prayer from the *Book of Common Prayer*, fitting with the week's theme (*BCP*, p. 816-817):

Everliving God, whose will it is that all should come to you through your Son Jesus Christ: Inspire our witness to him, that all may know the power of his forgiveness and the hope of his resurrection; who lives and reigns with you and the Holy Spirit, one God, now and for ever. Amen.

As we have said in previous lessons, sharing our personal stories builds deeper connections among group members. Your story may be exactly what another person needs to hear to encourage or strengthen them. And your listening to others' stories is an act of love and kindness to them—and could very well help them to grow spiritually. Begin your time together by using the following questions and activities to get people talking.

1. What has surprised you most about this group? Where did God meet, surprise or feel most present to you over the last seven weeks?

2. What has God been showing you through these sessions about what it means to live in community? Check in with each other about the progress you have made in your spiritual growth during this study.

EXTRA NOTE SPACE

....

....

....

....

....

....

....

....

....

....

....

....

....

....

....

....

....

....

....

....

....

....

WATCH *now*

DVD SESSION SEVEN

Watch the DVD for this session now. Use the *Notes* space provided here to record any key thoughts, questions or things you want to remember or follow up on. After watching the video, have someone read the discussion questions in the *Hear God's Story* section and direct the discussion among the group. As you go through each of the subsequent sections, ask someone else to read the questions and direct the discussion.

HEAR *God's* STORY

READ MATTHEW 5:16

In the same way, let your light shine before others, that they may see your good deeds and glorify your Father in heaven.

Use the following questions to guide your discussion of the teaching you just experienced in the video, and the Bible passage on the left.

1. Do you think of the word "call" as something that applies to all people or just to those people who feel a call to ordained or other parish ministry roles?

2. *Fr. Charlie asked, "What is the *it* in your life?" — or the work that God has given you to complete?

3. Do you ever struggle with a sense of your own gifts or calling? If, as the catechism says, our main purpose is "to glorify God and enjoy Him forever," in what ways are you doing these things?

NOTES

CALLING. The Father gave Jesus a specific work to complete. This work, His calling, was the Cross. Every Christian has a calling from the Father. In the teaching, Fr. Charlie said that each of us has a calling that is:

- *External* (originates outside of ourselves),

- *Personal* (specific to each one of us),

- *Compelling* (resonates deeply with us), and

- *A Choice* (we can choose whether or not to respond to it).

When you heard that four-part description of *calling*, what were some of the thoughts or images that came into your mind?

CREATE *a* NEW STORY

Think about specific steps you want to take to live a new story, to walk more closely with God so that you can be a part of His story, engaged in His kingdom.

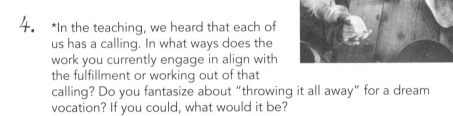

4. *In the teaching, we heard that each of us has a calling. In what ways does the work you currently engage in align with the fulfillment or working out of that calling? Do you fantasize about "throwing it all away" for a dream vocation? If you could, what would it be?

5. *What barriers (internal or external) are preventing you from "finishing the work you have been given to do"?

6. What choices are before you when it comes to the fulfillment of your personal call from the Lord?

7. How has God changed your story during this seven-week study? What new things is He asking you to do? What truth has transformed your heart?

8. If your group still needs to make decisions about continuing to meet after this session, have that discussion now. Talk about what you will study, who will lead, and where and when you will meet. Perhaps you would agree to go on to the next study in the Christian Life Trilogy, *The Resurrected Life.*

9. *What are the group's plans for attending Holy Week Services? Try to attend as many of the services your congregation offers.

10. *Review your *Small Group Agreement* on page 140 and evaluate how well you met your goals. Discuss any changes you want to make as you move forward. If you plan to continue meeting, and your group starts a new study (such as *The Resurrected Life*), this is a great time to take on a new role or change roles of service in your group. What new role will you take on? If you are uncertain, maybe your group members have some ideas for you. Remember you aren't making a lifetime commitment to the new role; it will only be for a few weeks. Maybe someone would like to share a role with you if you don't feel ready to serve solo.

11. Close by praying for your group's requests, and take a couple of minutes to review the praises you have recorded over the past five weeks on the *Prayer and Praise Report* on page 144. Spend some time just worshiping God and thanking Him for all He's done in your group during this study.

DAILY
DEVOTIONS

Continue on your journey through this week's Daily Devotions, found in *The Crucified Life* book. Each day, you will explore one aspect of the final word of Jesus from the cross: *It is finished.* As you do so, ask God to take you deeper into His word and help you more fully understand the power and purpose of living The Crucified Life.

APPENDICES

FREQUENTLY *asked* QUESTIONS

What do we do on the first night of our group?

Like all fun things in life–have a party! A "get to know you" coffee, dinner or dessert is a great way to launch a new study. You may want to review the Small Group Agreement (page 140) and share the names of a few friends you can invite to join you. But most importantly, have fun before your study time begins.

Where do we find new members for our group?

We encourage you to pray with your group and then brainstorm a list of people from work, church, your neighborhood, your children's school, family, the gym and so forth. Then have each group member invite several of the people on his or her list.

No matter how you find participants, it's vital that you stay on the lookout for new people to join your group. All groups tend to go through healthy attrition–the result of moves, releasing new leaders, ministry opportunities, etc.– and if the group gets too small, it could be at risk of shutting down. If you and your group stay active, you'll be amazed at the people God sends your way. The next person just might become a friend for life. You never know!

How long will this group meet?

It's totally up to the group–once you come to the end of this seven-week study. Most groups meet weekly for at least their first seven weeks, but every other week can work as well.

At the end of this study, each group member may decide if he or she wants to continue on for another seven-week study. Some groups launch relationships for years to come, and others are stepping-stones into another group experience. Either way, enjoy the journey.

What if this group is not working for us?

You're not alone! This could be the result of a personality conflict, life-stage difference, geographical distance, level of spiritual maturity or any number of things. Relax. Pray for God's direction, and at the end of this seven-week study, decide whether to continue with this group or find another. You don't usually buy the first car you look at or marry the first person you date, and the same goes with a group. Don't bail out before the 7 weeks are up–God might have something to teach you. Also, don't run from conflict or prejudge people before you have given them a chance. God is still working in you, too!

How do we handle the childcare needs in our group?

We suggest that you empower the group to openly brainstorm solutions. You may try one option that works for a while and then adjust over time. Our favorite approach is for adults to meet in the living room or dining room and to share the cost of a babysitter (or two) who can be with the kids in a different part of the house. In this way, parents don't have to be away from their children all evening when their children are too young to be left at home. A second option is to use one home for the kids and a second home (close by or a phone call away) for the adults. A third idea is to rotate the responsibility of providing a lesson or care for the children either in the same home or in another home nearby. This can be an incredible blessing for kids. Finally, the most common idea is to decide that you need to have a night to invest in your spiritual lives individually or as a couple and to make your own arrangements for childcare. No matter what decision the group makes, the best approach is to dialogue openly about both the problem and the solution.

SMALL *group* AGREEMENT

OUR PURPOSE:

To talk about what it means to live a God-first life with a few friends.

Group Attendance	To give priority to the group meeting. We will call or email if we will be late or absent. (Completing the Group Calendar on page 142 will minimize this issue.)
Safe Environment	To help create a safe place where people can be heard and feel loved.
Respect Differences	To be gentle and gracious toward people with different spiritual maturity, personal opinions, temperaments, or "imperfections" in fellow group members. We are all works in progress.
Confidentiality	To keep anything that is shared strictly confidential and within the group, and to avoid sharing improper information about those outside the group.
Encouragement for Growth	Accept one another as we are while encouraging one another to grow.
Shared Ownership	To remember that every member is a minister and to ensure that each attender will share a small team role or responsibility over time.
Rotating Hosts/ Leaders and Homes	To encourage different people to host the group in their homes, and to rotate the responsibility of facilitating each meeting. (See the Group Calendar on page 142.)

OUR *time* TOGETHER

Refreshments/mealtimes will be provided by:

The arrangement for childcare will be:

When we will meet (day of week):

Where we will meet (place):

We will begin at (time):

We will do our best to have some or all of us attend a worship service together.
Our primary worship service time will be:

Date of this agreement:

Date we will review this agreement again:

SMALL *group* CALENDAR

DATE	LESSON	HOST HOME	REFRESHMENTS	LEADER
Monday Jan 15	1	Bill	Joe	Bill

MEMORY VERSES

1

SESSION ONE: FORGIVENESS
Bear with each other and forgive one another if any of you has a grievance against someone. Forgive as the Lord forgave you.
(Colossians 3:13)

2

SESSION TWO: SALVATION
If we confess our sins, he is faithful and just and will forgive us our sins and purify us from all unrighteousness.
(1 John 1:9)

3

SESSION THREE: RELATIONSHIP
So you are no longer a slave, but God's child; and since you are his child, God has made you also an heir.
(Galatians 4:7)

4

SESSION FOUR: DISTRESS
Whoever drinks the water I give them will never thirst. Indeed, the water I give them will become in them a spring of water welling up to eternal life.
(John 4:14)

5

SESSION FIVE: ABANDONMENT
Hear my prayer, Lord; listen to my cry for mercy.
(Psalm 86:6)

6

SESSION SIX: REUNION
But I trust in you, Lord; I say, "You are my God."
(Psalm 31:14)

7

SESSION SEVEN: TRIUMPH
Each of you should use whatever gift you have received to serve others, as faithful stewards of God's grace in its various forms.
(1 Peter 4:10)

PRAYER & PRAISE
REPORT

SMALL *group* ROSTER

	PRAYER REQUESTS	PRAISE REPORTS
SESSION 1		
SESSION 2		
SESSION 3		
SESSION 4		
SESSION 5		
SESSION 6		
SESSION 7		

FAMILY *tree* EXERCISE

Every family has strengths. Unfortunately, every family also has wounds. Some wounds are the result of our bad choices, some are the result of the choices of others to harm or neglect, or to repeat patterns that were handed down to them.

Understanding the wounds not only in our own lives but also in the lives of our extended family will ultimately bring healing.

Take a look at the family tree on the next page. Begin at the bottom with your name, and if married, your spouse's name. (If divorced, insert your previous spouse's name, too.) Using the lists below, note any particular problems or wounds that you know you wrestle with. Do the same for your children, parents, brothers and sisters.

Continue up the family tree, filling in only what you know. Don't worry about what you do not know. Jesus will reveal what you need to know, and what He reveals He will heal. If you were adopted, again, fill in only what you know, and include both your biological family and your adopted family.

Some traumas may be healed through generational healing prayer without your knowing their exact cause. But the first step is simply awareness of the wounds your family has suffered.

On the next page is a partial list of common areas of generational bondage or sin. Which of these impacted people in your family? Ask the Holy Spirit to guide you, even to show you issues that may not be on this list.

VIOLENT DEATH OR SEVERE TRAUMA

Identify people in your family who:

- Committed or attempted suicide
- Were murdered or died in tragic ways (accidents, wars, drowning)
- Committed or participated in an abortion
- Miscarriages
- Died in prison or an institution, especially if they were alone
- Died without Christian burial or were unmourned
- Untimely deaths

HABITUAL PATTERNS OF SIN

- Adultery/fornication
- Incest
- Pornography
- Prostitution
- Sexual perversions or addictions
- Lust/Promiscuity

(We suggest you list all sexual partners and/or ungodly soul-ties you have with another. This is extremely important. You may be tied to that person spiritually, emotionally or mentally. You must name it to be set free.)

- Violence
- Racial or religious prejudice
- Anger
- Pride
- Murder
- Greed
- Arrogance
- Hatred
- Unforgiveness
- Addictions
- Abuse

- Hostility
- Control
- Manipulation
- Divorces
- Bitterness
- Revenge
- Depression
- Labeling a family member as "black sheep" or outcast
- Any involvement in the occult, Satanic rituals, connection with a witch

ILLNESSES OR DISEASE

- Arthritis
- Cancer
- Diabetes
- Mental illness or nervous breakdown
- Headaches

- Heart disease
- High blood pressure
- Respiratory trouble
- Skin diseases
- Ulcers

IN UTERO WOUNDING

-   Mother had a miscarriage or abortion prior to your birth
-   Child conceived in lust or rape
-   Illegitimacy
-   Parent considering adoption or abandonment
-   Difficult pregnancy (mother had trouble carrying child to term)
-   Life-threatening illness of baby or mother
-   Loss of father
-   Attempted/failed abortion
-   Ambivalence or rejection from either parent

HISTORICAL CONNECTIONS

-   Involvement with events of great sin, evil or trauma (massacres, slavery, etc.)
-   Non-Judeo-Christian origins in the family (Islam, Buddism)
-   Ethnic origin issues (negative traits, oppression, persecution)

After you have completed your reflection on your family tree, use your reflection and awareness to shape the content of your prayers, personal reflection and growth.

AS YOU PRAY:

-   Ask God in the name of Jesus to heal you of anything negative, harmful or evil revealed in your tree.
-   Seek the intercession of a trusted prayer partner or your small group.
-   Ask your pastor for spiritual guidance and resources.
-   You may want to participate in a generational healing service or participate in a Christian healing conference.
-   If needed, seek out the help of a Christian mental health professional.
-   Finally, use the Holy Week and Good Friday liturgy to leave anything not of God in your life at the foot of the Cross.

FAMILY *tree*

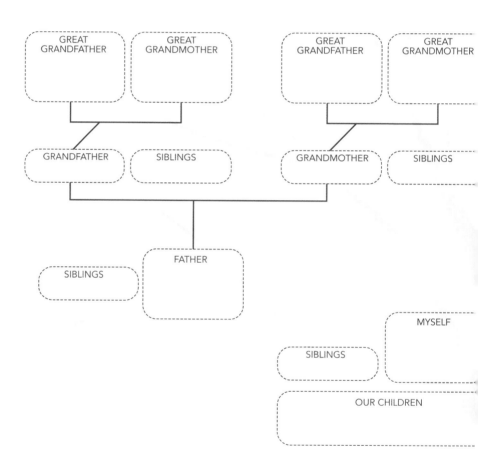

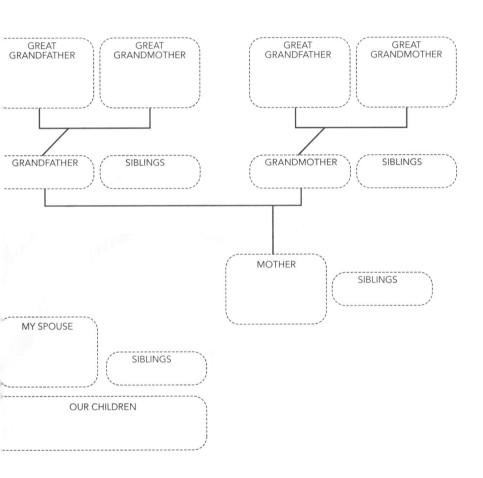

GREAT GRANDFATHER

GREAT GRANDMOTHER

GREAT GRANDFATHER

GREAT GRANDMOTHER

GRANDFATHER

SIBLINGS

GRANDMOTHER

SIBLINGS

MOTHER

SIBLINGS

MY SPOUSE

SIBLINGS

OUR CHILDREN

SMALL GROUP LEADERS

HOSTING *an* OPEN HOUSE

If you're starting a new group, or if this is your first time leading a small group, you should consider planning an "open house" before your first formal group meeting. Even if you only have two to four core members, it's a great way to break the ice and to consider prayerfully who else might be open to joining you over the next few weeks. You can also use this kick-off meeting to hand out study guides, spend some time getting to know each other, discuss each person's expectations for the group and briefly pray for each other.

A simple meal or good desserts always make a kick-off meeting more fun. After people introduce themselves and share how they ended up being at the meeting, have everyone respond to a few icebreaker questions, like: "What is your favorite family vacation?" or "What is one thing you love about your church/our community?" or "What are three things about your life growing up that most people here don't know?" Finally, ask everyone to tell what he or she hopes to get out of the study. You might want to review the Small Group Agreement and talk about each person's expectations and priorities.

You can skip this kick-off meeting if your time is limited, but an open house can help set your group up for success.

LEADING *for* THE FIRST TIME

Sweaty palms are a healthy sign.
The Bible says God is gracious to the humble. Remember who is in control. Those who are soft in heart (and sweaty-palmed) are those whom God is sure to speak through. God wants to use you exactly as you are to lead your group this week.

Seek support.
Ask your co-leader or a close friend to pray for you and prepare with you before the session. Walking through the study will help you anticipate potentially difficult questions and discussion topics.

Prepare.
Prepare. Prepare. Go through the session several times prior to meeting. If you are using the DVD, watch the teaching segment. Consider writing in a journal or fasting for a day to prepare yourself for what God wants to do.

Ask for feedback so you can grow.
Perhaps in an email or on cards handed out at the study, have everyone write down three things you did well and one thing you could improve. Don't get defensive; instead, show an openness to learn and grow.

Share with your group what God is doing in your heart.
God is searching for those whose hearts are fully His. Share your struggles and your victories. People will relate and your willingness to share will encourage them to do the same.

LEADERSHIP TRAINING *101*

Congratulations! You have responded to the call to help shepherd Jesus' flock. There are few other tasks in the family of God that surpass the contribution you will be making. As you prepare to lead, whether it is one session or the entire series, here are a few thoughts to keep in mind. We encourage you to read these and review them with each new discussion leader before he or she leads.

1. Remember that you are not alone. God knows everything about you, and He knew that you would be asked to lead your group. Remember that it is common for all good leaders to feel that they are not ready to lead. Moses, Solomon, Jeremiah and Timothy were all reluctant to lead. God promises, "Never will I leave you; never will I forsake you" (Hebrews 13:5). Whether you are leading for one evening, for several weeks, or for a lifetime, you will be blessed as you serve.

2. Don't try to do it alone. Pray right now for God to help you build a healthy leadership team. If you can enlist a co-leader to help you lead the group, you will find your experience to be much richer. This is your chance to involve as many people as you can in building a healthy group. All you have to do is call and ask people to help. You'll probably be surprised at the response.

3. Just be yourself. If you won't be you, who will? God wants you to use your unique gifts and temperament. Don't try to do things exactly like another leader; do them in a way that fits you! Just admit it when you don't have an answer, and apologize when you make a mistake. Your group will love you for it, and you'll sleep better at night!

4. Prepare for your meeting ahead of time. Review the session and the leader's notes, and write down your responses to each question. Pay special attention to exercises that ask group members to do something other than engage in discussion. These exercises will help your group live what the Bible teaches, not just talk about it. Be sure you understand how an exercise works, and bring any necessary supplies (such as paper and pens) to your meeting. If the exercise employs one of the items in the appendix, be sure to look over that item so you'll know how it works. Finally, review "Outline for Each Session" so you'll remember the purpose of each section in the study.

5. Pray for your group members by name. Before you begin your session, go around the room in your mind and pray for each member by name. You may want to review the prayer list at least once a week. Ask God to use your time together to touch the heart of every person uniquely. Expect God to lead you to whomever He wants you to encourage or challenge in a special way. If you listen, God will surely lead!

6. **When you ask a question, be patient.** Someone will eventually respond. Sometimes people need a moment or two of silence to think about the question. Keep in mind, if silence doesn't bother you, it won't bother anyone else. After someone responds, affirm the response with a simple "thanks" or "good job." Then ask, "How about somebody else?" or "Would someone who hasn't shared like to add anything?" Be sensitive to new people or reluctant members who aren't ready to say, pray or do anything. If you give them a safe setting, they will blossom over time.

7. **Provide transitions between questions.** When guiding the discussion, always read aloud the transitional paragraphs and the questions. Ask the group if anyone would like to read the paragraph or Bible passage. Don't call on anyone, but ask for a volunteer, and then be patient until someone begins. Be sure to thank the person who reads aloud.

8. **Break up into small groups each week or they won't stay.** If your group has more than seven people, we strongly encourage you to have the group gather sometimes in discussion circles of three or four people during the *Hear God's Story* or *Change Your Story* sections of the study. With a greater opportunity to talk in a small circle, people will connect more with the study, apply more quickly what they're learning and ultimately get more out of it. A small circle also encourages a quiet person to participate and tends to minimize the effects of a more vocal or dominant member. It can also help people feel more loved in your group. When you gather again at the end of the section, you can have one person summarize the highlights from each circle. Small circles are also helpful during prayer time. People who are unaccustomed to praying aloud will feel more comfortable trying it with just two or three others. Also, prayer requests won't take as much time, so circles will have more time to actually pray. When you gather back with the whole group, you can have one person from each circle briefly update everyone on the prayer requests. People are more willing to pray in small circles if they know that the whole group will hear all the prayer requests.

9. **Rotate facilitators weekly.** At the end of each meeting, ask the group who should lead the following week. Let the group help select your weekly facilitator. You may be perfectly capable of leading each time, but you will help others grow in their faith and gifts if you give them opportunities to lead. You can use the Small Group Calendar to fill in the names of all meeting leaders at once if you prefer.

10. **One final challenge (for new or first time leaders):**
Before your first opportunity to lead, look up each of the five passages listed below. Read each one as a devotional exercise to help equip yourself with a shepherd's heart. Trust us on this one. If you do this, you will be more than ready for your first meeting.

> Matthew 9:36
> 1 Peter 5:2-4
> Psalm 23
> Ezekiel 34:11-16
> 1 Thessalonians 2:7-8, 11-12

NOTES

NOTES

Artwork Attribution

Page 29, Jesus Carrying the Cross, c.1535, del Piombo, Sebastiano / Credit: Prado, Madrid, Spain / Bridgeman Images

Page 31, The Isenheim Altarpiece, c.1512-1516, Grunewald, Matthias / Credit: Musee d'Unterlinden, Colmar, France Giraudon / Bridgeman Images

Page 44, Garden of Eden, c.1555-1590, de Backer, Jacob / Groeninge Museum, Bruges / Bridgeman Images

Page 47, Adam and Eve in the Garden of Eden, c.1472-1526, Cranach, Lucas, the Elder / Credit: Kunsthistorisches Museum, Vienna, Austria / Bridgeman Images

Page 62, Christ on the Cross (oil on canvas), 1627, Rubens, Peter Paul / Koninklijk Museum voor Schone Kunsten, Antwerp, Belgium / © Lukas - Art in Flanders VZW / Photo: Hugo Maertens / Bridgeman Images

Page 65, The Tower of Babel, c. 1600, Marten van Valckenborch / Private Collection / Bridgeman Images

Page 80, I Thirst. The Vinegar Given to Jesus, 1886-1894, Tissot, James Jacques Joseph / Brooklyn Museum of Art, New York, USA / Bridgeman Images

Page 83, The Agony in the Garden, Boeckhorst, Jan (1605-68) / Private Collection / Photo © Agnew's, London / Bridgeman Images

Page 96, La Crucifixión, c. 1630, de Zurbarán, Francisco / Museum of Art of Ponce, Puerto Rico / Bridgeman Images

Page 99, The Agony in the Garden, 1502 (oil on panel), Carpaccio, Vittore (c.1460/5-1523/6) / Scuola di San Giorgio degli Schiavoni, Venice, Italy / Wikiart.org / This artwork is in the public domain.

Page 114, The Ghent Altarpiece: Adoration of the Mystic Lamb, c. 1432, Eyck, Jan van / Saint Bravo Cathedral, Ghent / Bridgeman Images

Page 130, Christ on the Cross, 1627, de Zurbarán, Francisco / Art Institute of Chicago, Illinois, USA / Bridgeman Images

Page 133, The Crucifixion, 1503, Cranach, Lucas, the Elder / Alte Pinakothek, Munich, Germany / Bridgeman Images

.